Pressing Memories

More than 100 years before digital photography outsourced our memories to the cloud, the middle and upper classes of 19th-century Europe looked to nature, not technology, to record the important moments in their lives. Largely the pursuit of women and girls, flower pressing was an art whose delicate beauty and emblematic floriography reflected the social and aesthetic sensibilities of the time.

Eleven-year-old Marie Luise 'Agnes' Leibbrand from Stuttgart was one such girl. As she vacationed with her family in southern Germany, Switzerland and northern Italy, or spent time with friends, admirers and loved ones, Agnes would collect samples of local flora to act as living mementos.

When her clippings of wildflowers, leaves and ferns were still fresh and free from dew, Agnes would press them between volumes of books or with a special field press. Once dry, Agnes bound them into neat arrangements and fixed the blooms to a piece of card or unfolded envelope, meticulously labelling each one with a number, date and description of origin. She would keep her floral memories in an ornate cardboard envelope box.

Between 1876 and 1890, just before analog photography became widely accessible, Agnes produced 42 of these pressings, weaving Europe's natural history with her own more personal one. I found the blue box with her pressed flowers in a drawer in my grandparents' house where it had been lying unnoticed for decades. Unfortunately, three of the cards have been lost to time, but what remains is a remarkably powerful account of youth, femininity, privilege and sentimentality in one young woman's life.

Agnes made the last entry in her floral diary on 16 May 1891. It is a branch from the bridal bouquet she held as she married Felix Steudel. Which is just as well, because had Agnes not married Felix, I wouldn't be here. Agnes is my great-grandmother.

Justus Oehler

Agnes Leibbrand
ca.1884

1.

circa 1876 von Herm. Lautenschlager.

circa 1876 from Herm. Lautenschlager.

Aus Maria Hölder's Gärtchen. 1880.

From Marie Hölder's little garden. 1880.

3.

Von Marie H. zum Neujahr 1882.

Von Marie H. zum Neujahr 1882.

From Marie H. on new year's eve 1882.

Aus meinem Bouquet bei Johanna's Hochzeit. 29. April 1882.

From my bouquet at (her sister) Johanna's wedding. 29 April 1882.

Aus Johanna's Brautbouquet 29 April 1882.

From (her sister) Johanna's bridal bouquet 29 April 1882.

6.

Vom Kayen bei Heiden 1883.

From the Kayen near Heiden 1883.

7.

Alpenrosen aus Kreuth. 1883.

Alpenrosen aus Kreuth. 1883.

Alpine roses from Kreuth. 1883.

Von Heiden 1883.

From Heiden 1883.

9.

Aus Heiden in der Schweiz. 1883.

Aus Heiden in der Schweiz. 1883.

From Heiden in Switzerland. 1883.

Blumen von d. Silberburg 1882. Gedörrtes Heidekraut aus Heiden 1883.

Flowers from the Silberburg 1882. Dried heather from Heiden 1883.

1883.

Aus Stachelberg.
(Schweiz.)

1883. Aus Stachelberg. (Schweiz)

1883. From Stachelberg. (Switzerland)

Edelweiß aus Kreuth u Moos aus Stachelberg. 1883.

Edelweiss from Kreuth and moss from Stachelberg. 1883.

13.

Aus Stachelberg.
1883.

Aus Stachelberg. 1883.

From Stachelberg. 1883.

14.

Aus Stachelberg in d. Schweiz.
1883.

Aus Stachelberg in d. Schweiz. 1883.

From Stachelberg in Switzerland. 1883.

15.

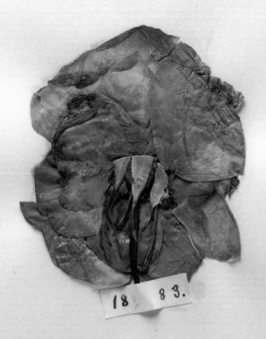

18 8 3.

Rothe Theerose von Frau Kessler aus Esslingen.

1883. Rothe Theerose von Frau Kessler aus Esslingen.

1883. Red tea rose from Mrs. Kessler from Esslingen.

18.

Corallenmoos.
Von Oscar Lauterbach. Aug. 1884.

Corallenmoos. Von Oscar Lauterbach. Aug. 1884.

Coral moss. From Oscar Lauterbach. Aug. 1884.

14. Januar 1884. (Aus einem Kranz.)

14 January 1884. (From a wreath.)

14. Januar 1884. (Aus verschiedenen Kränzen.)

14 January 1884. (From several wreaths.)

Von Helene Egelhaaf. August 1884.

From Helene Egelhaaf. August 1884.

Von Walter Schulz. im Bazar. 1885.

From Walter Schulz. in the Bazar. 1885.

Von Jean Back. Ruine Zavelstein. Juli 1885.

From Jean Back. Zavelstein ruin. July 1885.

Von Franz Seemann. Teinach. 12. Juli 1885. (Aus einem Bouquet).

From Franz Seemann. Teinach. 12 July 1885. (from a bouquet).

26.

Aus einem Bouquet, von Jean Back. 12 Juli 1885.

Teinach.

Aus einem Bouquet, von Jean Back. 12 Juli 1885. Teinach.

From a bouquet, from Jean Back. 12 July 1885. Teinach.

Rose von Freiherr von Vitzleben. Plättig. Mai 1890.

Rose from Baron von Vitzleben. Plättig. May 1890.

Von Alexander de Friderici. Page des Kaisers von Russland.
Juni 1890. Bürgenstock.

From Alexander de Friderici. Page to the Emperor of Russia.
June 1890. Bürgenstock.

Bürgenstock! Juni 1890.

Bürgenstock! June 1890.

30.

Bürgenstock.

Juni 1890.

Bürgenstock. Juni 1890.

Bürgenstock. June 1890.

Juni 1890. Bürgenstock - Rigi! (auf Kartenrückseite)

June 1890. Bürgenstock - Rigi! (on back of card)

Rigi-Staffel.
Juli 1890.

Rigi-Staffel. Juli 1890.

Rigi-Staffel. July 1890.

Andromea (chinesisch). Jasmin. Von Isola Bella!
Lago maggiore. Juli 1890.

Andromea (chinese). Jasmine. From Isola Bella!
Lago maggiore. July 1890.

34.

Myrthe u. Orangenblüte. Isola Bella. Lago maggiore. Juli 1890.

Myrtle and Orange blossom. Isola Bella. Lago Maggiore. July 1890.

*35.*

Oleanderknospe.
Erica.
Granatbaumblätter.
Japanesisches Gras.

Von Isola Bella.
Lago maggiore.
Juli 1890.

Oleanderknospe. Erica. Granatbaumblätter. Iapanesisches Gras.
Von Isola Bella. Lago maggiore. Juli 1890.

Oleander bud. Heather. Pomegranate leaves. Japanese grass.
From Isola Bella. Lago Maggiore. July 1890.

4bl. Kleeblatt. Isola Bella. Lago maggiore. Juli 1890.

4 leaf clover. Isola Bella. Lago Maggiore. July 1890.

37.

Von Isola madre! Juli 1890.

From Isola Madre! July 1890.

Alpenblumen v. M. Generoso. Juli 1890.

Alpine flowers from M. Generoso. July 1890.

39.

M. Generoso.

Juli 1890.

M. Generoso. Juli 1890.

M. Generoso. July 1890.

Alpenblumen Monte Generoso. Juli 1890.

Alpine flowers Monte Generoso. July 1890.

Alpenblumen v. M. Generoso! Juli 1890.

Alpine flowers from M. Generoso! July 1890.

42.

Alpenblumen: Monte Generoso! Juli 1890.

Alpine flowers: Monte Generoso! July 1890.

Aus meinem Brautbouquet. 16. Mai 91.

From my bridal bouquet. 16. May 91.

Agnes and Felix
circa 1893

Bürgenstock, Switzerland
Mountain located south
of Lake Lucerne

Esslingen, Germany
Town located near Stuttgart
or
Esslingen, Switzerland
Village located approx. 15 km
south-east of Zürich

Heiden, Switzerland
Village south of Lake Constance

Isola Bella and **Isola Madre**, Italy
Two of the Borromean Islands located
in the Italian part of Lago Maggiore

Kaien, Switzerland
1120m high mountain in the
Appenzell region

Kreuth, Germany
Alpine town located south
of Munich in Bavaria

Monte Generoso, Italy
Mountain of the Lugano Prealps

Plättig, Germany
Tourist destination in the Black Forest

Rigi Staffel, Switzerland
Summit in the Rigi Massif,
a mountainous region in central
Switzerland

Silberburg, Germany
Restaurant and popular destination
for excursions, closed its doors in
the 1930's

Stachelberg, Switzerland
Mountain situated in one of three
municipalities of the Swiss canton
of Glarus

Teinachtal, Germany
Picturesque valley located
south-west of Stuttgart

Zavelstein in Germany
Tourist attraction in the
Bad Teinach-Zavelstein region